"The eye never forgets
what the heart has seen"
— African Proverb

Abundant blessings for
your journey Kerri

As soon as I put the y in I knew it was wrong.

Me ke aloha pumehana

Michele   4/21/2025

Blissings
Kerri
(LOC)

paperblanks®
FLEXIS

Ce carnet aux motifs complexes capture l'essence des reliures en cuir finement travaillées de style Renaissance. Il reproduit l'art délicat du repoussage à l'or amené en Europe par les circuits commerciaux florissants avec l'Orient.

Auf diesem reich verzierten Bucheinband, der im Stil der kunstvollen Ledereinbände von Manuskripten der Renaissance gestaltet ist, sieht man die feine Handwerkskunst der Goldprägung, die auf den Handelswegen aus dem Nahen Osten nach Europa kam.

Questa copertina squisitamente rifinita si ispira alle rilegature in pelle rinascimentali e riporta in vita la raffinata arte della fregiatura in oro, una tecnica arrivata in Europa lungo le vie commerciali con l'Oriente.

Esta cubierta de sofisticada belleza captura el sabor de las refinadas encuadernaciones renacentistas en piel, y reproduce el delicado trabajo artesano del estampado en oro que llegó a Europa de la mano del floreciente comercio con las rutas del Este.

ルネッサンス期の皮表紙の味わいを再現。細やかに金色で施された細工は、交易華やかな頃に東方からヨーロッパにもたらされた金箔押し工芸。

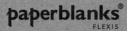

paperblanks®
FLEXIS

Ochre

Capturing the flavour of finely wrought Renaissance-style leather bindings, this intricately embellished book cover reproduces the craft of delicate gold tooling which was brought to Europe via the flourishing trade routes to the East.

ISBN: 978-1-4397-6542-5
MIDI FORMAT   240 PAGES   LINED
DESIGNED IN CANADA